P9-DFX-555

THE HIGH ROCKIES

Photographs and Text by George Brybycin

THE HIGH R

OCKIES

Special thanks to Monique Jeannotte, Barbara Belyea and Alf Skrastins for help and encouragement

ISBN 0-919213-72-3

DESIGNER, PRODUCER AND PUBLISHER: GEORGE BRYBYCIN

PRINTED IN CANADA

To my Mother

Foreword

I have always loved mountains. As each one of us presents a different face, so do mountains. All — from the Himalayas to the Alps to Mt. Kilimanjaro to Mt. McKinley — present a challenge. I have lived in many places but always in their proximity.

I owe my first knowledge of mountains to a dear friend of my father's, whom, as a child, I looked upon as a brave man of "iron will". He was the first to teach me the art of surviving in nature, the various ways of climbing mountains, and the observation of their many moods.

I have climbed mountains now for thirty years. I have a great respect for them and am very aware of the dangers they present. I never take them for granted or ignore their warnings. Coping with nature and the outdoors builds you physically and mentally; you acquire a kind of knowledge that no university can give.

Most of my escapades I do alone. I know that outdoor photography can be a very demanding and time-consuming affair. I crouch for long hours, sometimes numb with cold and hungry, but I wait patiently for I know my reward. It would be selfish, to say the least, to invite a friend on such trips. I prefer to share my experiences afterwards in a more comfortable environment.

The photos in this book are a major part of my life, and I feel privileged to be able to share them. My hope while selecting them for you was that they would convey my innermost feelings of fulfillment, happiness and peace.

In this book, I have linked together several thousand miles of trails. I am taking you on a gigantic hike that will embrace the entire North American Rockies, from the desert shrubbed lands of New Mexico, through Colorado's sand dunes and up its 14000-foot giants, into Wyoming's picturesque ranges and their wild game, under Montana's big sky, where some of the finest scenery in the Rockies can be found in Glacier National Park. Across the Canadian border, the horizon is different again. Among the challenging peaks of Alberta and British Columbia are found the first true glaciers. The western slopes are covered by a lavish and colorful vegetation, and game is plentiful. The hike pushes farther north, through the lovely, unspoilt wilderness of the Yukon, to end in Alaska where, close to your tent, wolf howls can be heard at night — a call of the North one can never forget. Huge mountains, vast glaciers, mighty rivers, lush valleys, crystalline lakes are all part of a fascinating beauty lit up by the torches of the northern lights.

Through the pages of this book, you will know the often uncomfortable nights I spent on top of rugged peaks. You will meet grizzlies, as I have, nose to nose. You may even catch the scent as well as the sight of alpine meadows covered with fragrant flowers and filled with exuberant life.

Heights have their own language. Theirs is not a silent world: streams, cascades, cracking glaciers, avalanches, electrical storms all join with the wind to remind you how small man is in this universe, but how mighty in his power to cope with his environment and find peace within himself.

CONTENTS

Anecdotes

In Colorado, there are fifty-five peaks or so that exceed 14000 feet. Many mountaineers endeavor to climb them all, and thus become members of the "14000 Footer Club".

The Maroons, one group of these peaks, are an arduous climb because of their steepness and heavy screes of rotten rock that seem to set you back two steps for every three you take.

In this area, I explored Crater Lake and the base of the Maroon Bells, where several mountaineers were carefully preparing their ascent. These two peaks, North and South, have been aptly nicknamed the "Deadly Bells", since every year people lose their lives climbing them. Even so, a large warning sign at the trail head does not deter others from attempting these peaks. I am always amazed, and encouraged, by the number of hikers and climbers in the United States.

My own target was Snowmass Mountain (14092 feet).

From Maroon Lake, I took the well-used Buckskin Pass Trail. Keeping south along the trail, I traversed steep slopes above Crater Lake, where I could admire the rugged west face of Pyramid Mountain standing silent just across the valley, and closer to me, the two masses of the Maroon Peaks.

As I went higher along the path, I came upon colonies of chirping pikas nestling among the boulders. These small rodents, in appearance not unlike miniature rabbits with short ears, are delightfully tame in this area. You can get very close to them; they simply go on munching little blades of grass that look like outsized green whiskers.

I went leisurely, taking many photos along my way; after three hours, I got above the timberline. Here I was treated to an unexpectedly beautiful sight: an alpine meadow opened before me, carpeted with an abundant variety of flowers. It seemed as if a rainbow had vanished in the meadow. I admit to being a great fan of close-up photography, so of course I could not resist stopping to catch the delicate beauty of these flowers.

I worked from one variety to another until my eyes watered from peering through the viewfinder of my camera. When I couldn't focus properly any more, I resumed my journey and just had time to see my goal on the horizon from Buckskin Pass before huge clouds hid it under a curtain of rain. At Snowmass Lake, some hikers invited me to dry myself by their campfire. This was a real pleasure, and a good break. In the meantime, the rain stopped; since it was only six o'clock, I decided to push on for another hour or two.

I followed the southern shore of the lake and eventually came to the steep avalanche slopes of Snowmass Mountain. My heavy pack was really weighing me down by this time. I wished for one thing only: a nice plateau where I could pitch my tent before night fell. I wasn't lucky. It was dark when, finally, I found a suitable spot to unload my pack, mount my shelter and enjoy a well deserved rest.

The joy of relaxing your body after a long day's climb is hard to explain. Although your limbs may ache, your mind seems more alert catching the quality of the peace and silence. Water rushing through the rocks gives you a feeling of well-being and contentment that makes you feel at one with the universe around you. I am happy in such surroundings: no city noises, no crowds, no pollution.

I was just sitting down to rest after my evening meal when I heard voices coming from behind some large outcrops of rocks. Curious, I walked towards them. To my surprise, I came upon a forest of tents sprawled all over the area. The voices turned out to be twenty-two Californians getting ready for an ascent of Snowmass. Their plan was to start at 4 a.m. to avoid the heat of the day. I didn't feel that energetic; I thanked them but declined their invitation to join them, and then went back to my tent. The night was cold, but I slept very comfortably.

The weather the next morning was fine; it would be a beautiful day. This gave me a boost, as a matter of fact, and I thought that I would try to catch up with my friends of last night, at least on their way down.

When I got to the base of the mountain and looked through my 200mm. lens [plate 13], there they were, but they were still going up! Apparently they had divided into two groups, the "experts" going to the left to tackle a more challenging slope, while the "intermediates" went to the right.

Once at the snowfields, I debated which way I should choose: there was a steep wall of granite in front of me and it looked mighty inviting . . ."What if I play a little trick on those guys," I thought, " and go straight up?" And so I did, and was up to the top in half an hour. I sat with the somewhat bewildered "experts", waiting for the other group to show up. The "intermediates" looked at me in disbelief when they arrived half an hour later. As a matter of fact, they seemed annoyed at my prowess.

Well, I can understand that. Yet after thirty years of climbing, I reckon that playing such an innocent joke on them was justified . . . Right?

There is a world of discovery awaiting a hiker. One has to be always ready to make a fast decision, to be prepared for any kind of eventuality and never to be disconcerted with the way a situation appears.

I had occasion once to be really startled, on an overnight trip to Storm Mountain, west of Banff, Alberta. I never thought that bears would travel very high up mountain slopes. After all, their food is found in lower meadows and valleys. I could see no reason for a bear to climb over 10000 feet just to have a look . . . but one did.

I had levelled off a small space in the thick scree where I pitched my tent. I wanted to catch the sunrise from the top of the mountain, so after setting my alarm for 5 a.m., I turned in right after sunset.

I slept soundly until I was suddenly awakened by a loud noise, like that made by large slabs of shale sliding over one another. My watch showed 4:45 a.m. Hikers? Already? It couldn't be. I peeked out of the tent and there, in the early dawn, was a large black bear, about fifty feet away.

I picked up my ice-axe, jumped out of the tent and stood awaiting the bear's next move. It seemed startled. Its nose stretched out, twitching, getting my scent, it balanced its head from left to right. Did it wonder if it were welcome or not, or was it deciding whether or not to start a fight so early in the morning?

Well, after a few seconds it must have decided that I was "barely" worth the effort. It circled my tent at a respectable distance and then ambled off.

Now, I have never thought of a bear as an enemy. But I feel that in this case I had a right to defend . . . the honey sweets and two chocolate bars that were in my tent.

Hiking in the mountains is bound to present some unusual, dangerous situations. My trip to Mt. Athabasca (11452 feet), in the Alberta Rockies, was very nearly my last.

I climbed Athabasca in about four hours, under the sun of a brilliant, cloudless August morning. But the summit proved to be disappointing. I barely had time to shoot a few photos before a sudden blizzard blew up: a whirl of snow enveloped me, and visibility was reduced to nothing. Resting was out of the question. I knew that the wisest thing for me to do was to start back without delay.

I managed to climb down to the north glacier without too much difficulty. There, the route becomes a passage across a narrow ledge, hemmed in between wide and deep crevasses and a steep slope, and skirted by blocks of hanging ice. This is the only way down. For two hours I probed about in the cold and blinding wind, trying to feel for the elusive passage, but to no avail. I couldn't find it. The wind was chilling and daylight had begun to fade. By this time I was close to exhaustion.

From past experience, I knew that the next best thing for me to do was to dig a hole and roll myself up in it. The storm had to blow itself away, and visibility would return. My lucky star was with me, for while I was hacking away at the ice, a last strong gust of wind blew the storm away, taking clouds and snow along with it.

I could see now that I had wandered off quite a distance from the narrow passage. I retraced my steps, still stiff with cold but feeling much happier.

Half walking, sliding, stumbling through the thick snow, I scurried down the slope. My going was now in complete darkness. I could see the lights of the cars on the highway below, and it was with a great sigh of relief that I finally stumbled, exhausted, into mine. I knew that it had been a close call.

This experience was an exception; such dramatic incidents do not usually happen to mountaineers. But by this anecdote, I want to emphasize the dangers of walking on glaciers. I recommend that such walks never be attempted by a lone hiker.

Those of you who have seen the North will understand my yearning to go back to that country. Time permitting, I would make it my holiday goal every year.

Some years ago, when travelling the Alaska highway was an adventure, I remember counting forty holes in my windshield. Now that the road is tarred for long sections, I counted only ten holes last year; I had no problem with shock absorbers, either!

On my first trip to the Yukon and Alaska, one region which I wanted very much to explore was the St. Elias mountains of southwestern Yukon. Although the Rockies officially end at the Liard River, the mountains belonging to the North American Cordillera system continue north to end in northern Alaska.

I parked my van near the southern end of Kluane Lake, in the Yukon, and scouted around the St. Elias mountains for a few days, in the hope of catching sight of some Dall's sheep. I didn't see any, but met with three grizzlies instead.

A few days later, on a sunny August morning, I set out on what I thought would be a three- to four-day hike to the impressive Kaskawulsh Glacier. My plan was to follow the west bank of the Slims River from the southern end of Kluane Lake, to cross the river at the glacier's tongue and then to climb Vulcan Mountain to the east. From there, I would get a bird's eye view of the entire glacier. And weather permitting, I could catch a glimpse of Mt. Cook, Mt. Vancouver and possibly Mt. Logan (19850 feet), the highest peak in Canada, lying seventy miles away.

My trail took me through endless marshes, broken up by steep slopes sometimes three hundred feet high. I had to climb these slopes, only to have to come down again to the river's edge on the other side. Twice I found myself bogged down in sinking sand: only by slowly lifting one foot out of the muck and placing it gently behind me, avoiding my previous footprint, did I manage to get back to firm ground. An energetic and time-consuming business!

On and on I trudged for long hours, noticing fresh bear droppings on my way. The sudden change in weather worried me also, for being about sixty miles from Yakutat Bay on the Pacific Ocean, this region is subject to changes in weather that come rapidly and without warning.

As evening approached, I decided to pitch camp above the treeline, away from curious bears. Once more, up a slope I went. Snow started falling as I put up my tent. Since there was no "sightseeing" to be done after my meal, I rolled up in the comfort and warmth of my sleeping bag. Ah! but not for long! A storm blew up which kept me awake all night wondering if the wind might not trigger a rock avalanche.

Morning brought little relief. The weather did not improve, making my walking all the more difficult in the fresh and heavy snow.

On I went, and at last reached the main moraine of the glacier. Here I faced a new problem. In order to reach Vulcan Mountain, to the east, I would have to either cross the river or climb the glacier and walk across it. Now, for a man alone, to do the latter would be most temerarious. I would have to cross the river.

The foot of Kaskawulsh Glacier presents a typical northern alpine topography: dozens of curving glacial streams, some deep and wide, growing into lakes of different sizes, all filled with water that freezes your toes in a matter of seconds.

I retraced my steps downstream for two miles, probing hopefully for a suitable place to cross. There was no suitable place — yet I hated to give up.

The weather decided the issue: it was raining heavily by now; I knew I had been beaten by the elements. I could only return to camp and hope for better weather the next time.

From this trip, I learned the hard way that to get to Vulcan Mountain, it is better to hike along the east bank of the Slims River and not the west bank, for reasons that are now evident.

I reached my van feeling a bit downcast. My achievements on this trip were . . . some fine blisters on my feet!

The North is still a vast, unspoilt region. Wild animals may cross the highway in front of a car, as did a cougar and a black wolf in front of my van. I went to Mt. McKinley National Park with the firm intention of taking all the pictures I could of the wild animals there.

Because of the risks involved in such an undertaking, park officials do not easily grant a wildlife photographer's permit. Obviously, one has to be most careful and on the alert in such wild country. As well as bands of Dall's sheep on the slopes of Cathedral, Iglo and Sable Mountains, there are large herds of caribou that migrate north to the Brooks Range in early summer, while dozens of smaller herds remain in the park year round. Moose and wolves can be seen at any time, anywhere, and so can grizzly bears: I have seen more grizzlies here in one day than I have seen in years down south.

When I began to hike in this wilderness, I was curious about the behaviour of the grizzlies. To my surprise, a ranger told me that there had not been any serious, unprovoked incidents involving the bears for several years. These comments on the bears' good behaviour didn't make me feel any better when I met three of them on a trail the next day. I simply backed away slowly, keeping my eyes on their humps, feeling better and better as the gap between them and me got wider and wider.

I explored the Polychrome Pass and Wonder Lake areas thoroughly.

I photographed magnificent Mt. McKinley under every angle and light possible, catching the almighty giant's reflection in ponds and lakes.

On a map of this fabulous region, I had circled Muldrow Glacier, just past Eielson, as my next hike. This mass of moving ice is one of the largest in Alaska, close to forty miles in length and exceeding three miles in width. The lower ten miles of the glacier are covered by rock and gravel brought down from the upper reaches, and vegetation has already established itself in places. The rugged mass of ice is pockmarked with huge cracks, cuts, holes, rivulets, rivers and small lakes.

I wanted to hike to Sunset Peak, near Anderson Pass, to get a view of the entire mass of the glacier. Little did I realize then that this trip would break records for me in more than one way.

Very early one morning, I left my van on the road just west of Eielson descent, and walked down to the Thorofare River. There dozens of little streams made it impossible for me to keep my feet dry. I took off my boots and waded the width of the river, one and a half miles. The going got better after I reached Glacier Creek and approximately three miles of open, flat meadows.

The path eventually narrowed between the glacier on my right and a steep wall on my left. Looking ahead, I took my bearing on three large boulders. Now there is nothing unusual about boulders in this area, but when I got to within a hundred yards of these, I examined them more closely by telephoto. Nothing unusual, I said to myself again, and continued on my way. But at fifty yards distance, the lightest rock seemed rather strange and I was sure it had moved somewhat. I stopped. Climbing a little knoll next to me, I shouted, whistled and clapped my hands. Only after ten minutes of listening to my antics did "the hairy rock" deign to raise its head and survey in my direction for a few seconds, only to drop its nose again and go back to sleep.

But that grizzly was on my very path. There was no way for me to go around it; it had to be moved from there. But how? An hour went by . . . the bear was still sleeping and I was getting impatient.

Now, there is a theory that claims that animals hate the smell of man. I wouldn't guarantee my method, but here is what happened in my case. Nature was on my side: after relieving myself, I saw the bear suddenly raise its head, catch the wind from my direction, quickly jump to its feet and scramble up the nearest slope. In a few seconds, it vanished. My trail was open.

My method had worked. Chuckling, I wasted no time, but moved ahead quickly. I had to make up for that lost hour . . . But I am still wondering!

I soon came to a vertical wall sloping down to the water. Again I had to cross the stone-cold glacier creek, my poor feet protesting.

At Anderson Pass, I decided to go straight up the west arm of Sunset Peak (7123 feet), immediately to the east of the glacier. From this vantage point, my view embraced the entire mass of Muldrow, from the north whence I had come, and up the ninety-degree curve to the west, where the glacier with its many arms runs for approximately twenty-five miles to the foot of silent, majestic Mt. McKinley, the highest point in North America.

I had accomplished this sixteen-mile hike over an elevation of 4000 feet in what was record time for me: seven hours, minus my hour session with the bear. It was an exhilarating feeling to be up there under excellent photographing conditions. I had to tear myself away from such enchantment.

At 4:30 in the afternoon, I started on my return journey. In the morning, my progress had been relatively easy over the frozen edges of the glacier and the creek, but now, after the warmth of the day, the melting glacier had raised the water level two to three feet. What had previously been a small creek had become quite a river.

I walked through cold streams every half mile or so. The sharp rocks on the river bottom made the going slow. If the crossing lasted more than thirty seconds, my feet were numbed by the cold. When I stepped out of the water, sharp needles shot through my feet and up my legs; it took me two to three minutes to get some circulation going, only to feel then as if my feet had been set on fire. This misery became part of the trip: there was no use complaining; I simply had to go on.

Although the daylight hours are long during the arctic summer, the length and difficulty of the trail forced me to hurry. Coming through the narrow gorge where I had met my bear in the morning, I started to sing and whistle to warn the fellow that I was on my way. There was no sign of it, however.

I was still a couple of miles away from my van when the sun set, at 10:30. I had another hour at least of twilight. By now my legs felt quite numb, and it was by sheer will power that I pushed on.

As I came up by the river where the ground levelled off, who should be waiting there for me? None other than that lazy bear I had encountered in the morning! Or maybe its friend? The day had been rough; I was tired and in no mood to play or argue. "What the heck," I thought. "You can have what's left of me, for all I care!" I just kept going straight on my way, right up to the bear. Casually I circled its mass, ignoring it completely . . . and kept on walking.

I stumbled into my van after possibly the most exciting and exhilarating single hike of my life. One never forgets such a day, such a challenge with oneself.

1

2

5

6

7

8

9

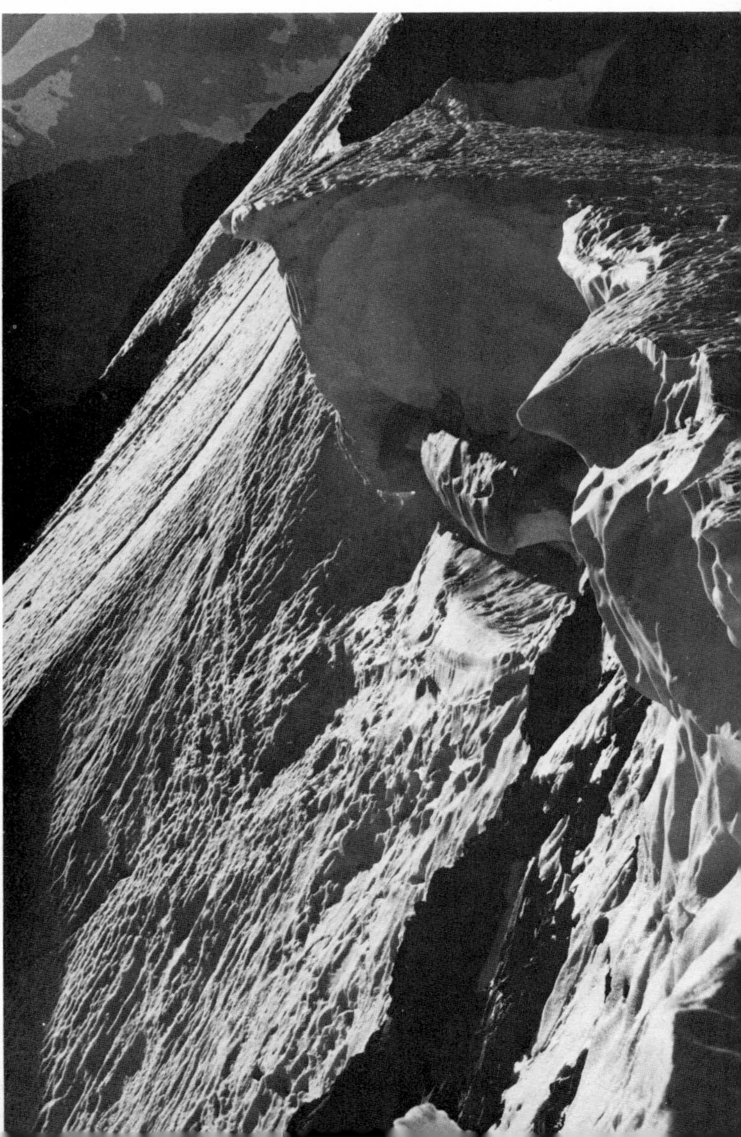

11

12

13

1

15

16

17

19

20

18

21

2

23

2

27

28

29

32

33

34

35

37

38

39

40

41

43

44

45

6

47

48

50

51

53

54

55

56

57

9

58

60

61

62

63

64

65

68

69

70

72

73

74

75

76

77

78

79

80

81

82

83

84

85

86

87

77

88

8

90

91

92

93

94

95

96

9

98

99

100

10

10

103

104

105

109

1

111

112

113

11

115

116

117

118

122

123

126

128

129

130

131

132

134

135

138

139

141

142

144

145

146

147

148

150

51

153

154

152

155

156

157

158

159

160

161

162

163

165

166

167

168

169

170

17

172

173

74

175

176

177

178

179

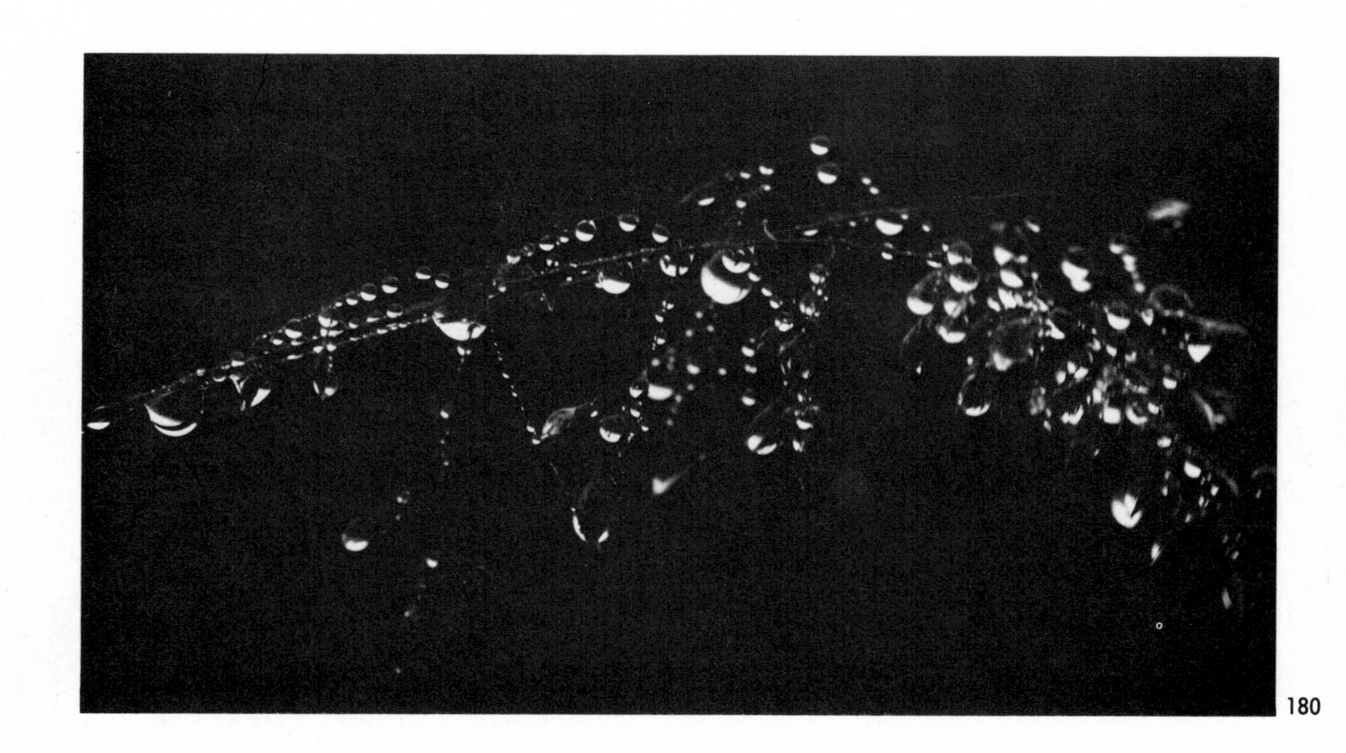

180

181

182

183

184

185

186

18

188

191

192

93

195

196

94

197

198

·01

203

204

·02

205

206

207

208

Notes on the Plates

Nigel Peak (10535) looming above North Saskatchewan River, Banff National Park, Alberta. (Front Cover)

Mountain Pond, Jasper National Park, Alberta. (Back Cover)

Robson River and Cariboo Mountains dominated by Mt. Sir Wilfrid Laurier (11750) British Columbia. (Pages 2 and 3)

Mount Athabasca (11452), Banff National Park, Alberta. (Page 4)

Glacier Lily (Erythronium grandiflorum). (Page 5)

Maroon Lake and Maroon Peaks, White River National Forest, Colorado. (Page 6)

Mountain Pond, Jasper National Park, Alberta. (Page 7)

1. The Great Sand Dunes. Great Sand Dunes National Monument, Colorado. These dunes were formed millions of years ago by sand blown by westerly winds from the volcanic San Juan Mountains. It was deposited on the San Luis Valley upon reaching the walls of the Sangre de Cristo Mountains. The dunes rise up to 700 feet above the valley floor. Medano peak dominates the horizon.

2. The Dunes and desert vegetation. The Sangre de Cristo Mountains in the distance.

3. Argenta Falls, close to San Cristobal Lake, south of Lake City, Colorado.

4. The Rio Grande Reservoir. Low water level during the summer.

5. A panorama of the San Juan Mountains, Colorado. Photo taken from Wind Point. From left to right: Redcloud Peak (14050), Red Mountain, Cristal Peak, Wetterhorn (14017), Matterhorn (13589), and Uncompahgre (14314), the highest peak.

6. Snowmass Mountain (14077), Colorado, viewed from Buckskin Pass.

7. A hiker's camp, west of Buckskin Pass. White River National Forest, Colorado.

8. Snowmass Lake from the granite slopes of Snowmass Mountain.

9. The Maroon Bells. Maroon Peak (14156) on the left and North Maroon Peak on the right, White River National Forest, Colorado.

10. Winter Magic.

11. A western arm of Grays Peak (14274), Colorado.

12. Alpine Willow: leaves after a morning rain.

13. Crossing a snowfield on Snowmass Mountain (14077), Colorado.

14. Cactus in bloom, New Mexico.

15. Latir Peak (12708), New Mexico, in a semi-desert brush environment. It is here, in northern New Mexico that the Rockies begin.

16. Spanish Bayonet (Yucca glauca).

17. Penstemon Nitidus, New Mexico.

18. Panoramic view taken from a peak directly north of Independence Pass (12095). La Plata Peak (14340) on the far left and Grizzly Peak on the right.

19. Goldflower.

20. Primula.

21. Around Independence Pass, Colorado.

22. Early morning fishing on San Cristobal Lake, San Juan Mountains, south of Lake City, Colorado.

23. Uncompahgre Peak (14314) in the San Juan Mountains, Colorado.

24. Rocky Mountain National Park, Colorado. The harsh environment is a cause of the death of many trees.

25. Picturesque view in Rocky Mountain National Park, Colorado. Longs Peak seen through the "window".

26. Group of California mountaineers on the summit of Snowmass Mountain (14077), Colorado.

27. A beauty amidst a rugged world.

28. Mt. Elbert (14433), Colorado. Highest mountain in the Rockies. Sheltered from the cold wind, mountaineers enjoying a well deserved meal. La Plata Peak (14340) on the left.

29. Alpine meadow on north slopes of Mt. Elbert, Colorado.

). Jenny Lake and the Teton Range. Grand Teton National Park, Wyoming.

1. Two kayakers on String Lake, Grand Teton National Park. Mt. Moran (12605) in the background.

2. The Snake River, Grand Teton National Park, Wyoming. The sun setting over the Teton Range.

3. An evening image of Mt. Moran and the Snake River.

4. Longs Peak (14255), Rocky Mountain National Park, Colorado. Various stages of the climbing.

5. Pearls of morning dew shot against the rising sun.

6. Jackson Lake and Mt. Moran. A night view from Colter Bay, Wyoming.

7. Jenny Lake. Grand Teton National Park, Wyoming.

8. After a rainfall: Dandelion (taraxacum officinale).

9. Cow moose in a forest clearing.

0. Bear grass (xerophyllum tenax).

1. Glacier Lily (erythronium grandiflorum).

2. Two hikers walking to Lake Solitude in the Teton Range, Wyoming.

3. The saddle of Grand Teton as seen from Middle Teton. Two climbers can be noticed in the lower right corner.

4. Grand Teton (13770). Highest peak of the Teton Range. Two mountaineers are crossing the glacier.

5. Resting on the trail to Lake Solitude, Teton Range.

6. Purple Cranesbill (Geranium viscosissimum).

7. Alpine flowers.

8. Grand Teton National Park, Wyoming. A girl hiking over a snowfield. Trail to Solitude Lake. South-west face of Mt. Moran in the centre.

9. Teton Range in the rising sun. Grand Teton National Park, Wyoming.

0. Early morning in the Rockies.

51. An incredible spectacle of autumn colors.

52. Lower Falls of the Yellowstone River, 308 ft., Yellowstone National Park, Wyoming.

53. Raccoon (procyon lotor).

54. Canyon of Yellowstone River with Lower Falls in the distance, Yellowstone National Park.

55. Early morning on Yellowstone River, Yellowstone National Park, Wyoming.

56. Two bull moose browsing near a lake in the early evening. Yellowstone National Park, Wyoming.

57. Close up photos of nature.

58. Doe Mule deer resting on a warm summer day.

59. Coyote and magpies feeding on the carcass of a deer. Yellowstone National Park, Wyoming.

60. Clements Mountain (8774), towering west of Logan Pass (6649), Glacier National Park, Montana.

61. A lush alpine meadow surrounds Mt. Reynolds (9125), with Glacier Lilies on the foreground. Glacier National Park, Montana.

62. Morning mist in McDonald Creek Valley, Glacier National Park, Montana.

63. St. Mary Lake. Glacier National Park, Montana.

64. Autumn image of Flathead River, Flathead National Forest, Montana.

65. Winter in Montana.

66. Crocus (Anemone occidentalis).

67. Swiftcurrent Lake and Mt. Wilbur (9303). Glacier National Park.

68. A spectacular Montana sunset.

69. St. Mary Lake, Glacier National Park, Montana.

70. Autumn image of Flathead River, Flathead National Forest, Montana.

71. St. Mary Lake, Wild Goose Island in the centre. Glacier National Park, Montana.

72. Crowsnest Mountain (9138). A landmark in the southern part of the Canadian Rockies, east of Crowsnest Pass, Alberta.

73. The Three Sisters (highest peak, 9634). Well known landmark east of Banff, Alberta.

74. East face of Mt. Louis (8800), as seen from the slopes of Mt. Cascade, near Banff, Alberta. Mt. Fifi on the right and Mt. Edith on the left. A paradise for rock climbers.

75. A family of mountain sheep basking in the hot summer sun.

76. Lake Minnewanka, from Cascade Mountain. On the right, the Fairholme Range and Mt. Inglismaldie. Banff National Park, Alberta.

77. Common Yellow Paint Brush (castilleja septentrionalis). Found in higher altitudes throughout the Rockies.

78. Bear Grass (xerophyllum tenax). Blooms every seven years, reaching heights of over 3 feet. Found in Glacier National Park, Montana and in Waterton Lakes National Park, Alberta.

79. Mt. Eisenhower (9076). Formerly known as Castle Mountain. A familiar landmark in the landscape west of Banff, Alberta.

80. Mt. Rundle (9838). Named after a methodist missionary, Robert Rundle. Most photographed mountain in the Canadian Rockies, landmark of the Banff townsite.

81. Ski jumper "flyes" over Mt. Rundle, Banff National Park, Alberta.

82. Growing in popularity sport: hang gliding.

83. Red-tailed hawk. Bird of prey common to many regions of the Rockies.

84. Rocky Mountain Tick or Wood Tick. Common pest in all regions of the Rockies, mostly found on sunny lower slopes. Active from May until mid-July. Can cause Rocky Mountain fever.

85. German wasp.

86. Doe deer resting on a warm summer day.

87. Bobcat (lynx rufus), browsing through a meadow.

88. Telemark. A growing in popularity annual cros country ski race in the Lake Louise area, Alberta.

89. Numa Mountain (8941), B.C. In the Vermilic Range, accessible from Floe Lake.

90. A southern unnamed neighbor to Mt. Verendrye in th Vermilion Range, eastern British Columbia.

91. Rocky Mountain Goat (oeramnos americanus). sure-footed white hair mammal, found mainly in cen tral and northern Rockies.

92. Insect on a wild flower.

93. Ptarmigan shedding its winter camouflage.

94. Mt. Ball (10865). Ball Range, west of Banff, Albert

95. Ptarmigan Lake at sunrise in the shadow of Redoul Mountain, north of Lake Louise, Alberta. View fro Fossil Mountain. Frozen Redoubt Lake in the left co ner.

96. Waterton Lakes National Park, Alberta, general view

97. Lineham Lake viewed from the slopes of M Lineham, Waterton Lakes National Park, Alberta.

98. Mt. Eisenhower (9076). Banff National Park, Albe ta.

99. Moraine Lake, Banff National Park, in the glory the rising sun.

100. Victoria Glacier. Immediately west of Lake Louis Alberta. A very well known and attractive glacie Accessible from Lake Louise or from Lake O'Hara vi Abbot Pass (9588), where a cozy alpine hut is locate Note the three climbers descending from the Glacier

101. Mt. Lefroy (11230). Dominates the south-we skyline from Lake Louise, Alberta.

102. Mt. Victoria (south peak: 11365, north peak 11116). North-west of Abbot Pass, one of the mo beautiful but dangerous mountains in the area.

103. An ice climber from Spokane, Washington.

104. Skiers on a practice slope with the picturesque Mitche Range in the background, Eastern British Columbi

5. Mt. Bourgeau (9615), west of Banff, Alberta.

6. Mt. Assiniboine (11870). Early morning reflection in Magog Lake. The highest peak in the southern Canadian Rockies. Often referred to as the Canadian Matterhorn.

7. Mt. Temple (11626). Second highest peak in Banff National Park, located five miles south of Lake Louise. The north face of this mountain is considered a real challenge for climbers.

8. Early morning in the Valley of the Ten Peaks. Bow Range, Banff National Park, Alberta.

9. Bald Eagle (haliaetus leucocephalus). Well known for its strength and exceptional vision. Adults develop white, fully feathered head and white tail. The wing span can reach up to seven and a half feet.

0. Ptarmigan Lake at sunrise in the shadow of Redoubt Mountain, Banff National Park, Alberta.

1. Hikers meet with horseback riders near Ptarmigan Lake.

2. The Cat family: Cougar, Adult Bobcat, Kitten Bobcat, Canada Lynx.

3. Grizzly bears mating.

4. Rugged peaks of the Vermilion Range, British Columbia, reflected in a mountain pond.

5. Lavish beauty of nature.

6. Takakkaw Falls. Yoho National Park, British Columbia. An outlet of the southern end of Waputik Icefield.

7. Takakkaw Falls in their impressive winter silence.

8. A bear crosses a mountain torrent, using a fallen tree as a bridge.

9. Cathedral Crags (10083) to the right and Cathedral Mountain (10464) to the left. West of the Kicking Horse Pass, Yoho National Park, British Columbia.

20. Mt. Stephen (10495). Directly east of Field township. Here, in September of 1887, J. J. McArthur made history by being the first man ever to climb above 10000 feet in the Canadian Rockies.

121. Summit of Mt. Temple (11626). Banff National Park. Well earned breakfast. The Horseshoe Glacier below.

122. Mt. Ball (10865) aglow in the dying sun. Banff/Kootenay National Parks.

123. Cathedral Crags (10083), in the glory of the rising sun, Yoho National Park, British Columbia.

124. Mt. Hector (11135), lone mountain 12 miles north-west of Lake Louise. A bivouac near the summit.

125. Climbing up Mt. Hector (11135). First going through lower slopes of golden larch trees, then through rocks and snow, to reach sheer ice on the last part. The summit provided one with a breath-taking view of the area.

126. A solitary climber's camp on Storm Mountain (10372). Mt. Ball (10865) on the right. Banff National Park.

127. Rising sun from the summit of Mt. Hector. From the left: Mt. Lefroy, Mt. Victoria and Mt. Goodsir.

128. Summit of Mt. Hector. Looking west, Hector Lake and Waputik Icefield.

129. Peyto Lake, a gem of the Banff National Park.

130. Bow Lake and Bow Glacier in full summer gala, Banff National Park.

131. Mt. Chephren (10715), also called the Black Pyramid. Banff National Park, Alberta.

132. Howse Peak (10793). Waputik Mountains, Banff National Park.

133. Moose (alces americanus). Large mammal of the deer family. Commonly found from northern United States to Alaska. Feeds mainly on aquatic vegetation. Photo from Bow Pass, Banff National Park.

134. Observation Peak (10414). Rises directly north of Bow Pass, 28 miles north-west of Lake Louise. The north face of the mountain is covered by a large snow-field and glacier. Panorama of mountains looking south-east. Mt. Hector (11135) on the right.

135. Peyto Lake, Peyto Glacier and Wapta Icefield, seen from Observation Peak.

136. North face of Observation Peak (10414). Banff National Park, Alberta.

137. Peyto Lake, from Observation Peak. Banff National Park, Alberta.

138. The Vermilion Range from Numa mountain. Kootenay National Park. Frozen Floe Lake below.

139. Mt. Sarbach (10350), North Glacier. North part of Banff National Park, Alberta.

140. Mt. Athabasca (11452). An eastern sentinel of the Columbia Icefield. One of the most popular mountains with climbers, photographers and sightseers.

141. Athabasca Glacier. A tongue of the Columbia Icefield which along with the Clemenceau Icefield forms the largest body of ice in the Rockies.

142. Wilcox Mountain (9463), Jasper National Park, Alberta.

143. Nigel Peak (10535) and North Saskatchewan River. Banff/Jasper National Parks, Alberta.

144. Mt. Sir Donald, Glacier National Park, British Columbia. A paradise for rock climbers.

145. Portrait of elk.

146. A vast panorama of mountains looking south from Mt. Athabasca. Mt. Bryce (11507) in the centre with part of the Saskatchewan glacier on the left corner below.

147. North face of Mt. Bryce (11507). East glacier of Mt. Andromeda on the foreground.

148. North glacier of Mt. Saskatchewan (10964).

149. Mt. Athabasca (11452) and its north icefield. Border of Banff/Jasper National Parks, Alberta.

150. Athabasca Glacier: a spectacle of nature, Jasper National Park.

151. Two Massachusetts climbers reaching the summit of Mt. Athabasca (11452).

152. Columbia Icefield as seen from Mt. Athabasca (11452). Mt. Columbia (12294) dominates the horizon.

153. On the Silver Horn, Mt. Athabasca. The Columb Icefield provides a spectacular background.

154. Reaching the Silver Horn, west peak of Mt. Athabasc (11452).

155. Marmot (murem montis).

156. Timber wolf (canis lupus).

157. Red fox (vulpes vulpes).

158. Moose (alces alces).

159. Bird's eye view from the summit of Nigel Peak wit Mt. Andromeda (11300) to the left. The Athabasc Glacier on the right.

160. Nigel Peak (10535). Located directly north c Sunwapta Pass on the border of the Banff/Jasp National Parks. A most rewarding view of M Athabasca (left) and Mt. Andromeda (11300) righ can be enjoyed from this point.

161. A meadow after a rainfall.

162. Wild flowers.

163. The Canadian Monarch: Mt. Robson (12972) in i autumn glory. Mt. Robson Provincial Park, Britis Columbia.

164. Helmcken Falls, Wells Gray Provincial Park, Britis Columbia.

165. Spahats Falls, Wells Gray Provincial Park, Britis Columbia.

166. A January spectacle.

167. Mt. Robson (12972), highest mountain in the Cana dian Rockies. Glorious January sunrise.

168. The Peace River: a flowing giant of the North.

169. The Liard River, northern B.C. Geographical end c the Rocky Mountains.

170. White Thistle (cirsium hookerianum).

171. Goat's Beard (tragonogon dubius).

172. Mountain goats. A familiar sight in the Rockies.

173. Mule deer peering into the camera.

4. Common Blue Bell (campanula rotundifolia).

5. Western Anemone (Anemone occidentalis).

6. A young bald eagle trying its wings.

7. Black bear: a skillful tree climber.

8. Arctic Wolf: a majestic prowler of the North.

9. A young grizzly bear trying to beat the summer heat.

0. A northern beauty after a rain shower.

1. Robertson River, in eastern Alaska, looking south.

2. Mule deer buck.

3. Mt. McKinley (20320), the peak that native Alaskans have always called DENALI, meaning The Great One. Mount McKinley National Park, Alaska.

4. The lush vegetation of the tundra in contrast to the desolate ice capped mountains, Alaska.

5. Nelchina Glacier sandwiched between the Chugach Mountains and the flower covered tundra.

6. Early morning reflection of Mt. McKinley in a tundra pond. Mount McKinley National Park, Alaska.

7. A night scene in Mount McKinley National Park, Alaska.

8. A new day rises at the Wonder Lake campground, Mount McKinley National Park, Alaska.

9. Band of Dall's Sheep on the southern slopes of Sable Mountain. Mount McKinley National Park, Alaska.

0. A caribou family caught by the camera on the tundra.

1. A hardy nomad: caribou (Rangifer arcticus) scaling a ridge.

192. Grizzly bear (ursus horribillis). Quite common in the North; there remain about 20,000 of them in North America.

193. Alaska Range, dominated by Mt. Hayes (13832). Photo taken in early morning from Big Delta.

194. Portage Glacier in the Kenai Peninsula, southern Alaska.

195. Dall's Sheep. Found only in the Yukon and Alaska.

196. Rare sight: An Arctic Wolf.

197. Thorofare River. Mount McKinley National Park, Alaska.

198. Lower portion of Muldrow Glacier as seen from the western slopes of Sunset Peak. Mount McKinley National park, Alaska.

199. Upper part of Muldrow Glacier, looking west. Mount McKinley on the horizon.

200. Ice capped peak, south of Anderson Pass, along the eastern edge of Muldrow Glacier. Mount McKinley National Park, Alaska.

201. Arctic fox. Found in the Yukon, Alaska and the High Arctic.

202. Red fox. A familiar sight throughout Alaska.

203. Three ptarmigan chicks in their summer camouflage.

204. Two caribou (Rangifer arcticus) by a tundra pond.

205. Bald eagle (haliaetus leucocephalus).

206. Morning image of Mt. McKinley and surroundings.

207. Bird's eye Primrose (primula mistassinica).

208. Mt. McKinley (20320). The highest mountain of North America. North face. Morning reflection in Wonder Lake.